Along the Bronzing Lanes

for Ali – with Best Wishes.

Along the Bronzing Lanes

poems through life

Sandra MacGregor Hastie

Sandra MacGregor Hastie.

SMH BOOKS

British Library Cataloguing in Publication Data

A catalogue record for this book is available from the
British Library

ISBN hardback 0 9512619 6 7

First published April, 1994, by
SMH BOOKS
Pear Tree Cottage, Watersfield, Pulborough
West Sussex, RH20 1NG

Typeset by
Inkwell, Cocking, West Sussex

Printed and bound in Great Britain by
Hillman Printers (Frome) Ltd

for my sister
Helen Jean Hastie,
who died in infancy
and thus knew nothing of
the joys and sorrows of this life;

for Roy MacGregor Hastie
- friend and brother -
who has just died
and who knew *all* about them,

and

for my beloved sister
Pat Downs,
for her care and kindness.

Cottage life has much influenced my writing, which began at the age of seven.

I was born in Manchester but, when in 1940 a bomb neatly removed the house next door, my father moved us to Tanglan Cottage, in Pen-y-fford, a small village at the foot of the North Welsh hills. The cottage was too small for three growing children and their parents and the garden, too large to manage. But I loved many things there. There were apple trees to climb up, raspberry-cane 'forests' to hide in with a fire of sticks on the path, and a billy can bubbling with water for a secret tea. And there was a huge pear tree straddling the roof of the shed at the bottom of the garden.

Travelling widely (London, Spain and France have been the most important *places* in my life) I learned much, and wrote on it.

At nineteen, I stood in the grounds of an East Grinstead cottage (although a very grand cottage) and told my very dear Godmother, Kay Waddington, that one day I would live in Sussex, and have four children. I did both, in reverse.

Two of my children were born in Dublin, two, in London, where we lived until 1992...

All through my life, I have worked hard, doing the things I wanted to do, so far as possible. My headmistress at The Queen's School, Chester, told my mother when I was fifteen that I would 'flit like a butterfly through life, from daisy to daisy'. My mother was indignant, but the great Miss Maclean was right. But whatever I have done, I have always come back to working with books - editing, publicising, publishing - writing. And to quote Edward Elgar (who quoted from John Ruskin's Sesame and Lilies) at the end of the original score for *The Dream of Gerontius*, this collection of poems is, I believe, 'the best of me... this, if anything of mine, is worth your memory'.

And here I am in West Sussex in springtime. The birds are still chirruping for me - from dawn, the garden provides much of the food I eat, a rather ragged honeysuckle bush nestles against the window of the kitchen, where I work, and the cat and dog console me for children grown-up and gone. Where could I be happier than in Pear Tree Cottage, Watersfield?

April, 1994

CONTENTS

Tanglan Cottage

The wooded way

A mossy path through the wood;
a leafy way through the trees;
a mirrored pool in the mud;
a heavy storm with the breeze.

A clump of firs in the thorn;
a bramble climbing the bark,
and through the still air is borne
the sweet song of a lark.

A tangle of bracken gold;
a holly bush by young ferns.
The winter sunlight streams cold.
The lark blithely returns.

A blue and a thin sky
beyond the branches' pattern.
And rusten carpets lie
where the grasses sadly flatten.

1949

In such a night

O, the sweet stillness of a summer night -
the unobtrusive glances of the moon;
the moths that fumble softly in their flight;
the honeyed softness of the air in June;
the roses (red reflections of the sun);
the daisies and white dew upon the grass;
the sharp-eyed hares that in the hedges run;
the showers that gently come and swiftly pass.

Summer is queen of all the seasons: fair,
and night - end of the day; sweet time of peace.
And summer nights. With what do they compare?
Let there remain at least the thought of these.

June, 1951

The child apart

They all went on ahead,
leaving me the empty picnic basket
to carry after.
But I didn't mind.
Carefully they took with them their laughter;
they gathered up the vestiges
of merry conversation,
and left me there, alone.

I heard their feet
tusselling with the wood's undergrowth,
their final voices' echo over the slope,
and I sat back,
putting the things together;
slowly emptying bread crumbs out of the paper bags;
burying abandoned crusts in the bracken's
golden arms ready to receive the bread
for birds and insects,
now my sole companions.

And I didn't mind, I didn't mind.

I was alone. They will not come back now,
I said to myself, I hope.
They are gone.
As always they have gone on ahead,
leaving me the basket
to carry after.

Sans maman

The fire dies, soot settles in the grate.
The room is coated with ash and dust.
Creamy walls are bleak, the door is barred.
Curtains lean limp against the sullied window panes.
Pots line the sink. The teapot, cold, stands full.
The clock ticks on (each minute is an hour).
Lights go out. The house becomes a shade:
a heavy shadow in the shapeless night;
a misty silhouette in the thick sky,
and nestles down, and droops in gloomy sleep.

As the sun comes up over brown hedges,
the sky takes on a friendlier, red glow,
like a blue face that reddens with running.
The clocks go off. Two heads make sudden movement
above their eiderdowns. A hand gropes desperately
for the shutter-off of the cold alarm.

When the newspaper is hurled at the door
both groan, fumble for clothes, dash out of bed -
banging themselves, braining themselves
on something they forgot to move
the night before.

Now the house is hit with unhappy feet.
The fire is lit, goes out, glows again.
Shoes become shinier, hearts grow happier,
The Two grow dappier, and lean on the fire.

There is a sound like the mixing of cement,
and Father is there, clutching his teacup,
newspaper and curved-stem pipe.
He fills the kitchen, and The Two disappear
in a flurry of shoehorn, smoke, and Father.

Breakfast collapses.
Father and The Two catch the bus to Chester.
The house is left alone...

Now
the dryads and the nymphs are about.
Pots shine like new paint, the fire grins wider.
The kitchen suddenly is clean.

Someone has returned.

She sits in the Big Chair, and drinks tea
with an elegant smile that shows she is pleased.
The doting dog chews his tail
with occasional glances at her.

The Two have returned, and Father,
and they flutter round the Someone,
like eager butterflies round a red daisy.
Much tea, more talk, smiles, and memories
of dull, dark, desolate mornings
and fireless kitchens at night;
no meals waiting;
no-one to break up wrangling scenes,
and make the house a merrier place;
no-one to darn a sock or wash a glove
and, most important of all,
no-one to love.

Examinations

There is foreboding in the sullen sky,
sombre grandeur above the leaves,
filling the magnetised mind with fear...

'Break the seal on all books!'
We need knowledge, yes, to know life.
But in the search, fancies grow rife...

How green under the boughs!
The nettle-filled heart of the willows.
The sheltered bank of the river.
The sad-salty look of the pool.
Soft rushes in whispering water
churned by the Tourists' Atrocity.
The red stillness of sunset.
The grey gloom of twilight.
And the blackness of bats in the night.

No, we must concentrate!
In two weeks...
dead faces, dithering hearts, dry mouths, hot hands -
a room of printed sheets and blank paper,
of misgivings and the looming of fate.
And in the minds of all,
foremost, is sweat.

Life looms
in lifeless, stifling rooms.
Examinations...

The impenetrable hood

What is happening now?
I am forgetting friends,
and all I used to live for.
The milk I drink from the fawn cow
turns to gall. My faith bends.
What is happening to me?

I am wearing the Impenetrable Hood;
I cannot see.

But at night
the Hood falls,
and life becomes ecstasy.
The dead-day stars shine through me,
the river runs rippling over my bones,
cats rend the air with their caterwauls.
My uncertainty goes when the moon is about.
I walk sure-footed in the darkness,
putting by the past,
postponing the future,
and forgetting my groans.

Shine! shimmering slender stars.
Shine! Mars.
Blaze! moon, from the half-light.

The river depths are clear now.
Night!
Come, sweep away the day's might,
and keep away the day's mud,
that I may feel fall from my brow
the day's doubt:
the Impenetrable Hood.

Lavender sickness

If I were clever enough to imagine
sweet smells to take away the taste of snow,
I should look hard, hard for lavender trees,
with my eyes closed,
feeling a syrupy wind blow
along the hedges. And a hot sun.
I should see soft blue flowers, and drink their perfume,
and put my hands among them, and my face,
rubbing my cheeks and my longing palms
in lavender,
the soft blueness of lavender,
sweet lavender.

The escapist

Carry me, call me to green darkness.
let me lie on the softness of grass,
warmed and fragrant and full of sun.
Let me live in quiet lands
where the river's song is a comforter.
Let me sing my heart's joy,
where the weeping trees sweep the water.
Let me smell the good earth; the salt pool.

Let me - escapist and coward -
sink into life outside life,
forget I am, and live
in fairness and frivolity,
in awareness and oblivion.
Let us, together, dress ourselves for dancing;
clothe ourselves in romance,
and in the awe of God's stillness
Which seeps into the beginnings of night,
Let us whisk the world from our sight.
O my love, let us forget.

The poppy song

If I were told my life were done
except for three moments more,
that of last wishes I had but one
to ask and not bargain for,

I should not ask for friends to fawn
around in these minutes three,
nor relatives to mourn -
no death-bed gathering for me.

My past? I want not to recall
happy or hopeless days;
when nothing but love mattered at all;
the 'modern' or 'moonstruck' phase.

And nor, sadistic at the core,
as many people I know,
should I crave keys to the future's door
to see, perhaps, man's overthrow.

I should ask for summerness;
sun, and the feel of a silk dress;
a stool with cushions pink;
and a sleepy poppy drink.

And, among long, supple grass,
with my back against a tree,
to hear the drowsy insects pass,
listen for a droning bee,

smell the smiling lavender,
touch its crispness with my fingers;
feel Nature's soundless purr
that in all summer lingers.

Day for Milton

I was reading a book,
a poem by Milton.
The pains I took to read it,
and the time it took to read each page!
I blinked
and tried to concentrate.

Half-past eight!

A piece of wood fell out of the fire.
I grew warm, I was tired...
"What did Milton think of Marvell?
What did Cromwell think of...?"
The rain wrangled In the ringing gutters.
The book became a meaningless block
before my eyes.

Nine o'clock!

Turn on the news to hear
what Churchill said,
what Bevan cried,
and who has died.
The news...

What a comfortable place is bed!
White sheets and black darkness.
How white the pages,
how black Milton's sonnets are!
Milton wrote the Areopagitica...
How smooth and clear the ceiling is -
smooth and soft...
crisp...clean...cream...

In bed, Milton's soul
softens in his poetry.
I sleep, and all that I have read
becomes a mere dream...

Today I read a poem by Milton.
The meaning was not blurred.
I knew how he felt,
and what made him write each word.

Snowdrops for my mother

(i)

I have held up snowdrops to you in a mittened palm,
a school scarf round my ears and a satchel on my arm.

I have brought these white, nostalgic tears of flowers and,
smiling, put them by you, with a larger hand.

I have left my typewriter on a January day
to seek the florist's snowdrops, or steal some on the way.

Eagerly and happily, from Christmas to the spring,
the snowdrop search inspires me more
than the first birds that sing.

And although I live in Kensington, many miles from home,
I knew today, instinctively, that Snowdrop Time had come.
I will send a bunch to someone who, alone, will understand
they are more than small white flowers from a florist's on the Strand.

Snowdrops for my mother

(ii)

White, pretty, ashen ghost flowers
behind the shop's glass,
how could I ignore you,
not buy you, just pass

to work again, and worry,
of ways of eking out,
take up life's crazy hurry,
like a somersaulting trout?

I shall have this bunch,
no matter what it costs to buy,
to send off to you
who will smile at them, as I.

Poems for a soldier

(1)

Our love was never said.
And now that I believe you to be dead,
it calls, cries out in me,

so that I make this late confession
to your spirit:
I loved you.
I loved your face, your hands,
the way you smiled when I thought
you were going to be grave.

I loved your love of clichés:
'Cheery-bye' and 'All the best'. 'Must fly'.
'Ah well, that's that, there's nothing to be done.
No use crying over spilt milk'.

Our love was never said,
only implied in many different ways.
The passion was sealed up
inside a haze of conventions
we had no time to break.

Our love, never said,
now cries out, calls out in me,
now that I believe you to be dead.

Poems for a soldier

(2)

Under the sad willow tree, memory,
it came to me
that we would never talk this way again,

You would laugh,
wouldn't you?
if you could hear these thoughts of mine
as words in a hollow sadness
spoken across the sea to to where you lie?

Or, in a star already,
under wet earth marked with an ill-made cross
quick-contrived by a luckier, grim-faced man,
perhaps you lie,
impervious to my thoughts and premonitions,
under the sorrow-shaken willow tree.

For Michael

I decided this was an evening meant for walking,
full of the smell of rain, and rain on grass;
radiant skies; no rancour in the wind -
and an horizon of pure golden glass.

Seduced by the evening's beauty then,
I came at length upon a succulent slope
of golden-syrup ferns all steeped in storm,
treacherous and steep, and slippery as wet soap.

And suddenly, I was filled with a fine, formless pleasure
to feel again the same tranquillity
(blinded with a burst of memories...
laughter in the wind from you and me)
as when we walked here all those years ago,
in the full, calm silence of sure friends.

I shall reflect, I know, on few moments
harmlessly happy as these when the world ends.

Brown touch

We have no need of the moon
to love, nor a single star,
nor crave stimulation from a tune,
poignant twanging of one guitar.

Nor do we need a language of love
of this or other lands.
Your eloquence for me is in
the brown touch of your hands.

Bruna carezza

Non abbiamo bisogno della luna
per amare, ni de una singola stella,
ne sollecitiamo lo stimolo di un melodioso
ossesionante suono di ghitarra.

Neppure abbiamo bisogno di un linguaggio
d'amore, o d'altre contrade -
la tua eloquenza per me e
nella bruna carezza del tue mani.

Brune caresse

Nous n'avons pas besoin d'une si belle lune
pour nous aimer, ni de la moindre étoile,
nous ne voulons pas non plus aviver notre ardeur
avec la musique poignante d'une guitare.

Il ne nous manque non plus une vraie langue d'amour
ici ou ailleurs. Il n'y pas de besoin.
Ton eloquence pour moi, je peux bien la trouver
seulement dans la brune caresse de tes mains.

Shirt music

Tomorrow in the same sordid room
(cream walls grime-glazed, beer advertisements
the frayed ends of curtains, barely hidden;
cheap cigarette butts in bits of beer froth,
and fish and chip shop mists
wrapping the light bulb in ghoulish gloom),

but one day from tonight
this yellow, stuccoed ceiling
of no outstanding master
will hide us both
from raven skies or rainless starlight,
nor will it matter which.

I shall sit here and sear
your face-form with my greedy glance,
and of this seething slime magnetism
feel nothing.

In a trance,
how well you knot your tie, I'll think,
and in spite of this dark dirtiness
how clean you look.

I'll like your latest shirt.

Dark doubt

For twenty minutes fully we've been parted -
drastic delay between our timeless kisses.
And even in such short time dark doubt has started:
I wonder which the other truly misses?

Dualogue on the Point

Who would line a smooth, untroubled brow?
Who would breed the right amount of discontent?
to make a brain ferment
with thoughts long since begotten and forgotten?

Stay still. Lie still.
Watch the sky with the moon in it.
This is not a time to answer questions.

But if it were
would I be justified in what I want to say?
some men like limp, disordered scarecrows
litter the world; being born
yet lying on, as seeds
unswollen and oblivious of outcome
in a firm, warm, uncompromising womb.
It is ironical that they would see -
if they but cared to look -
their outcome not disillusionment,
nor fear, nor agonising hazards,
just years linking hands
until the dull chain is complete

Stay still. Lie still.
Wonder at the enlarged pupil of light
that is the moon with the sky round it.
This is not the time to analyse men's destinies.

Yet if It were the time....
There are some wrenched from the womb;
forced to make an untimely journey.
Dazed and ill-equipped
they set up camp in unsuitable places,
finding always they are too late
for the best sites;
resigned to defeat without bitterness,
because defeat is a common companion,
often spoken of, like daily bread.

Stay still. Lie still.
The moon has gone.
Pinned on the breast of the grey Highland sky
is the sun: an orange medal.
The purest beauty comes
in sudden, unexpected moments;
as did the sun, out of the moon,
notice this beauty now.

Among the other left are those
who almost bear themselves,
so eager their hearts and eyes
to know beyond the dark
there fellow lives and men
and to search, and find, perhaps,
so that their cry may be:
"We have looked! At least
we have looked!"
If there has been small relief
at least our souls have grown
and bodies strengthened with expectancy.

Stay still. Lie still.
Light like a pair of scissors
cuts sea from sky
with one, long moment.

But are you not glad
there are those
(a few, but not chosen)
whose lives are not their own?

They are halved, like the Saint's cloak,
for charity and peace of mind
They are quartered, like martyrs,
for their ideals and dedication,
They are split into thirty pieces of silver
for a reward that is not always claimed.

Stay still. Lie still.
The sun, more polished yet,
glitters above us in the pale, metallic sky.
The Point gleams with wet heather,
and the rocks around us shine
like sharp-chinned demons.
Islands, dreams in the mist,
lie delicately in the water.
Look at all this and feel
that silence would be the best thing.
Lie still.

London

Like wings, Roy

Parents are funny things.
Like wings, Roy,
they have the means
to carry and fly their children,
but they do not always try.

And when their children
want to try,
at first they find
alone they cannot fly.

Persistence shows them, though,
that, without wings,
the sky is possible.

Star-conscious

I have never seen so many stars,
like diminished lights of cars,
but paler than yellow -
the colour of Yale keys.

It is long since I noticed how bright
they are: Bond-Street jewels,
accessories to night,
not garish,
but glittering and resplendent.

Strange, when I see
these silver caskets of stuff like dew,
suspended in the black sky,
I remember, as a child of three
(always wanting to know why),
I asked if the brightness of stars
was the clue
to brightness in a night.
No-one answered me.

It is long since I noticed how bright...

The bed-sitter

tick tock
tick tock
just listen to the clock
tick tock-ing on the shelf
tick-tocking
and myself
just looking
at the clock
tick-tocking
on the shelf

tick tock
tick tock
the night draws on
and my fire burns low
no use looking
for a shilling
for the gas
(tick tock)
for I have none
neither do I know
anybody in this house
I can ask
I can go
to no door
in this house
tick tock
not knowing anybody
tick tock
tick tock

tick tock
I would like some tea
hot tea
or milk

hot milk
tick tock
they say
it makes you sleep
(if only I could sleep)
but it seems
these days
that sleep
is not for me
and in bed
all I hear
is the clock's
tick tock
and the time
hurries on
and I lie
just thinking
and tossing
and thinking
while the clock
(tick tock)
on my shelf
just repeats
tick tock
tick tock
you are all by yourself
tick tock
tick tock
tick tock

You are all by yourself
tick tock
tick tock
tick tock
tick tock

Paeonies

When I was a child
I played among paeonies,
crimson and correct.
I tried to make them wild.
I pulled at the petals
to make the flowers frayed,
but they stood, unperturbed
and straight-stemmed as I played.

When I was past ten
The mirror summoned me.
I looked, and was bored,
and looked there again.
I decided to dye red
my hedge of flaxen hair.
I did. Once more I looked -
but the same face was there.

And now I am older
I want to change the world,
I have independence.
My thoughts become bolder.
I have altered my living,
my trying, my eating,
my joking and jeering,
my sudden way of giving.

I have to stay alive
so I meditate on money
(for like everyone, a poet
needs a purseful to survive).

I watch other people
and wonder if they feel
they would like to stop the traffic;
cease the whirring of the wheel.

But cars go on killing
and wheels never stop,
and I still buy my bread
at the same local shop.
My face has changed little,
flaxen still grows my hair.

The paeonies grow straight
in the old garden there.

One more espresso

Through the wide window my friend can be seen,
dark head bent over the Gaggia machine;
seeming intent on the coffees that stream
into the cups, through a station-like steam......

Beaches of Italy -
brown skins, and bare;
sand strewn with bodies;
sand in my hair;
cold drinks and hot sun,
and all my friends there.

Behind the counter my friend mops his brow,
Still coffee comes (it's eleven: faster now).
Swiftly the liquid with froth finds its way
into cups - on to tables - to mouths. Pull away!
coffee's consumed all the long night and day.

Brothers in Italy,
how do you fare?
(Wine and warm evenings,
no coats, and no care.)
Waiting for English girls,
foreigners' flare!

Under the strip light my friend can be seen,
venting his wrath on the Gaggia machine.
- Jobs for Italians aren't easy to find,
but work on this monster? I'm out of my mind!

Blue skies of Italy.
Heat in the sun;
walks on a soft beach
when daylight is done.
Fine, fine, my Italy,
you warned me. You've won.

Midnight is coming. My friend, think again.
Rest for a moment. Count up to ten.
Stop running your hands through dishevelled hair.
- What haven't we here that you have over there?

Waves, blue like cornflowers;
blue skies; and brown eyes
in dark, sun-tanned faces;
laughter and sighs;
brown skins, and bare.
And all my friends there.

Even the spiders sing

Normality has got them,
normality is there,
normality's the swear word
only the young don't swear.

A balance of perception,
a soft spit at the vile,
a nailing up of passion -
just hand me down that phial.

I can't take the acceptance,
to hell with compromise!
He who can cry, laughs deepest.
Reason all, and he dies.

Give me the stirring sickness
that's underground in spring.
Let me shout out of context.
Even the spiders sing.

Theatre women

They come in shoals: stoles draped; hair scraped,
brilliantined back in deliberate waves.
Powder chokes their skins; black, their mothy lashes;
their sickening perfumes mingle in the fur-filled foyer.

Almost as if they didn't want to, they climb the stair,
settle without interest into their box or circle seats.
And can I read pleasantness in their looks
that swoop like birds, relentless-winged, down and round?
No! I hear 'great heavens, what some women wear!'
'Good lord what some people *wear*!'
'*Who's* that freak in black?'

The orchestra's thin strings hint
of actors leaving their greasepaint dens;
on the stage, grotesquely poised, ready
for Act I ('and I hope to hell they like it'!)
And the woman next to me - no lady -
is trying to take possession of the arm of the seat;
slowly she slides her snake-like arm over the plush,
silently stakes her stupid claim,

The play's over, 'Thank the lord for that!'
says someone fervently.

Of all the looks and leers, remarks and movements,
no-one has said anything tonight sincerer than

'the play's over, thank the lord for that!'

Spain

What is life?

Life is no dream
- who said it was? -
nor anything so close allied
to unreality.

It is not for one to plunge into,
tired and looking for
the misty archway to enchantment.

Nor is it enough to lunge for life:
frail fingers, sweating with effort,
graze only the velvet beauty
of an hour of escape.

A man can neither pray -
for life is not a common prayer,
the due of a holy man
who asks and asks all night,
cold-kneed with supplication,
in the simple quiet of his room,
expecting the reflection
of a simple answer.

Life is the full grey pitcher
of frothing crimson wine
on our common table,
so full and potent,
full of potentialities,
that why should men resist
the drink that laughs in the veins?

And he who, like a fool,
not understanding,
pushes the fair jar from him
with a cold hand,
will miss the smiles
and sudden clarity,
the climaxes of joy
and love and sinless, liquid ecstasy
that beat in the heated blood
throbbing in the body
that recognises.

Alicante
1957

Fragment

Oh that there were some small justice
in the world I could believe in,
that I could turn my back on a friend
and go on trusting him,
confide my secrets and share problems
other people might solve better than myself,
oh if I could find one man I could trust
like a child, I would smile in
the face of the world's tragedies.

In the middle of a vast, grey desert
tiring to the eye to look for horizons,
a child found itself alone with a man.
They examined each other carefully,
with slanting glances, as strangers do,
who are not sure of the outcome of
a relationship forced upon them.

It is a strange place, thought the child,
and there is nobody here I know.
I am a long way from home
and I don't know which way it is.
And if it were not for this man
I should be quite alone.
I am a long way from everything I know
and the warmth connected with familiar things
and there is only this man
with an unfamiliar face
who looks quite kind, but I don't know him,
and I wonder what he is thinking about.....

This is a strange world, the man thought.
Odd things happen and here I am
suddenly in a strange place
with a child as my only companion.
She is completely lost.
I am lost, but
I think I know the best thing to do.
There are always oases in a desert, it's just a
matter of knowing where.
I have been in stranger places, and I
have always found a solution to my problem.
But this child -

The man and the child continued to
contemplate each other
until night made their faces and
their expressions indistinguishable.
It was natural for the child to feel sleepy.
It was natural for the man to take her
upon his shoulder, and let her sleep
in the warmth of his jacket, while he
continued working out the best plan.

The days went slowly on, like a procession
of time, along the way through the desert.
When the sun began to scorch her shoulders
he walked with his coat over her.
When it parched her mouth, he stooped
and wet her lips with the precious water.
When she muttered about hunger,
he gave her a little bread.

And each time darkness came, and
she shivered and was frightened,
he took her up on his stronger shoulder
and she fell into trustful sleep.

Alicante
November, 1957

A method of forgiveness

I went into a church.
It was the first time for a long time
and it was strange.
But they had said:
if you go into a church
and talk to God,
it will clear your head.

I sat down
and waited for something to happen,
But nothing but the flap
of my impatient glove
against my bending knee
bridged the gap
between the living
and the seeming dead.

It was cold and black
and misty as charcoal.
Nothing...

Eventually, impatient,
I said to God:
- Look, excuse me,
but I must talk to someone,
and You are the best person
I can think of.
Excuse me if You are busy,
with more important things...

- No, thinking it over again,
(in this tense, empty silence)
why should You listen to me?
You have so many things to do.
You are more occupied, I imagine,
than the busiest of businessmen.
Why should you listen to me?

I waited.
There was no clear answer.

- All right, I said.
Look, forget about it.
I told them it would be
a waste of time.
I said, what could you possibly
have to say to me?

- You are the complete
and glorious opposite of me,
the example I can never follow,
the rock I can never climb,
the song I can never sing.

Here where the green gloom
of an unknown, foreign
church of God, settled between me
now at the steps
and Him at the altar,
I felt the silence change.

There was a stir,
like the rebirth of an idea
in the air;
a noiseless shuffle of dust,
restless. And I remember clearly
feeling uneasy
and as if unborn.

I listened, hard now.
God seemed to say:
- You talk a lot of nonsense
for one who has lived
quite long enough
to know better.

I see so many sinners
that you are nothing new
nor unusually shocking.
Just another cause of sadness.

But I am God.
The significance of this
must truly penetrate
and remain with you,
if you are to see
eye to eye with Me.
I am God,
and I love,
and I forgive.

I knelt on the altar steps,
too moved to cry,
so close to Him.

Forgive me, Lord,
my doubt.

Alicante
24th January, 1958

Psalm of the twentieth century

God, who exists beyond the television aerials
on the yellow roofs,
God, who exists for me,
God, who exists for those
not beguiled by the clever arguments of intellectuals
and men too sensitive to logic,
for the un-self-sufficient -
perhaps the simple-minded,
I am aware
You are not inaccessible.

Accessible! Blessed accessory to life
(for me, at least)
and yet the essence of it; the nucleus of every atom,
the centre of conception.

God, who exists beyond the television aerials
on the yellow roofs,
the chimney-pot extremities of houses,
I can see you in a straight line
from where I sit on my carpet
drenched by the effective, orange heat
of this room's, every room's, gas fire.

Beyond the roof, the aerials, pylons,
God, who exists for me,
who exists,
I am aware.

Moments by the sea

We were not faced with any problems
sitting in the sun, our warm skins
beginning to be the colour of honey,
like the sand.

The fine day's end was hours away.
When the sun's bloom faded,
we would see the summer moon.

My hair was heavy with salt water,
like seaweed.
There was a purple sail on the sea's back.

And that and this is all that I remember:
I looked at you -
you were smiling without thinking.
I had to look away.
Wind from the water touched my shoulder,
and I shuddered.
Perhaps you wondered why,
for when I looked again
you were not smiling.

Travelling

These were not wasted points of our existence -
when we left home, bidding friends goodbye,
watched our boat quickly forget the harbour,
and turned away from England without a sigh.

This was no stupid use of our years' span:
a fulfilled desire to roam the South of France;
visiting Chamonix, Paris in April,
Venice by moonlight; seeing a Spaniard dance.

We did not squander those days in the mountains,
meeting strange people and making them friends,
asking for two cabbages in a foreign language.....

for we thought back at the evening-ends
to crumpets in the firelight; Mamma and her mongrel;
avid magazine perusal each Thursday night;
the smell of the lilac and sun-warmed apples;
in bed, watching that flashing beacon light.
Things once taken for granted we yearned for,
coveting old routines more constant than the sun.
And oh, that daily scramble in an alien porch for letters,
the reassurance ringing in "love from everyone"!

Back in London

Entry into the heart

Into my heart
tender and unprotected
by a lining
experience should have been provided,
you crept last night.

You crept so gently
that I was unaware
of any entry.

Only now
that the touch of your hand
is a thing of the past
and a thought of the future,
I feel you inside me
and cry with the joy of it.

Don't go from my heart.
You belong there.

Lying in bed

Lying in bed
in a darkness
that only tends
to clarify my thought,
I turn on the pillow
and try to catch the sound of you
locking the doors downstairs,
carrying our glasses with a clink-clink
into the kitchen,
pacing the lounge,
crossing the hall,
closing your door for the night.

It is ten minutes since
we stood uncertainly
before the fire.
"Good night," you said,
"sleep well."
"And you, sleep well," I said.

And then
I just came up to bed.

After an unexpected evening

Tonight is like a badly painted picture -
jarring of ideas, mingling of temperaments,
mixture of glittering paints and dark paints of fears,
display of aesthetic doubt and confidence.

But the canvas -
underlying, indispensable,
thought or tool necessary to take an idea,
is no longer of importance.

Background smothered in a whirl
of inefficient, all-concealing hesitation.

Jarring of ideas covers the smothered canvas,
provocative
to the eye of the discerning artist.
Tonight? - yes, a badly painted picture.

Only the artist shows promise.

Sleep, like an insidious shadow...

There is still so much to do tonight,
to say and write,
and there is now so little time.
Sleep, like an insidious shadow,
creeps slowly over me,
intruding on my working mind,
superimposing will on yielding will.

I have so much to say,
but the sands are beating me.

And so the scripts that need revision
and ideas to be edited
I'll put now to one side,
and think on that
which needs no concentration:
my love for you.

Love, you have never been discarded,
nor filed away. Our passion, never pending,
burns till it's spent, and then burns again.
And no amount of work or sleep
can creep up on our love; obscure it.

Still, sleep is trying hard
and with an effort now
I softly recite my creed of you,
clasping my hands unconsciously,
smiling towards my bed.

I love you, I believe in you. I trust you.
Oh dear, my need for you
like sleep, is slipping nearer.

Apologia

After this night
how can you make
apologies?

now that the morning stars
with their far beauty
have resigned themselves
to slight appreciation,
and the poplars shimmering
in the new dawn sun
accept a mere glance.

For we have found
a fresh reason to wonder.
We have found, each in the other,
the last, lost part of you and I.

Why should you make apologies?

Imagine this:
imagine that
you stand up on a hill
in high summer.
Do you apologise to the soft grass
your shoe disturbs
and mercilessly tramples?
Do you
cry sorry to the sun
because you wear a hat against its heat
and glasses to stave off the blinding glare?

Do you voice deep regrets
to each small animate thing
you know is lying in the turf -
the cricket singing and the soft-eared rabbit
watching you move,
because you do not seem to notice them?

And is it guilt you feel
at a sudden interest
in the warm blue sky
that makes you look disdainful of the hill
and all it holds?

Imagine all this,
and laugh
into an obscure cranny of the mind
apology.

Love song at night

Oh, how I love you!

thinking at night, and in the sun,
how soon our hours were run,
and spent themselves as onlookers to passion.

Our passion has mingled curiously
with peace of mind.
And I suppose time was tolerably kind;
her hired-out hours, our temporary slaves,
were loyal, silent friends,
were sympathetic, though they could not stay.

Oh, how I love you!

Now words alone reverberate
on minutes; the empty husks of hours
that are serving other lovers.

All I have left to do
is let my sad self-pity
evaporate in tears.

Oh how I love you!

For Ezra

Why did we pursue it, when we knew it had to end?
When, at the beginning, when both our heads for spinning,
there seemed nothing for the winning, and Time was
not our friend?

Was it just the thought, perhaps, of something unachievable?
We could have just part of it, and want in vain for more.
Did we not think that we'd regret moments irretrievable,
Unspeakable - ah well, all's fair in love and war!

(Mixed thoughts are fair, and moods, and emptiness,
in love and war.)

So why did we pursue it, when we knew it had to end?
Why weren't we both content to say: "Just let me be your friend"?

Just let me be your friend!

I've so many memories of sunny days, and stormy days.
Weather didn't matter, did it, whether we'd wet feet?
Who could ever think of love, be far too near the brink of love,
and the next moment blink and say:
"There's thunder in the air"?

 And, ah well, if mothballs fell, we weren't the ones to care.

Now I am just tired, not of thinking about you,
but thinking of our happiness,
our happiness and healthiness, and all we tried to do:
our laughter and our longing; the man you noticed scrounging,
the sixpence that you gave him, and my smile - though we knew
to pursue our love was fruitless if we put an end in view.

I have tidied up my reasoning. I know that what we had -
so short and so exciting, leaving time for little fighting,
for whims and little games, the affectations at love's door
(though all's fair in love and war) -
was something more than an affair, a meeting and a parting,
a little time we had to share, then sighs...a tear or two -

It was a reassurance that we needed, you and I:
that when we give we gain by it,
not hoping to obtain by it.
Our hearts are filled with pleasure and our souls,
with warmth and light.

Joy

Were we waiting for joy, you and I?
Did we think it would arrive on a plate,
that it would assail us, soon or late?
And it could never pass us by,
could it?

Yes, it could.

Cold shoulder us?

It did -
left us within whirls of worse misery,
lepers incurable.

In creamy skies of dreams,
tangible, untouchable,
joy, in voluminous petticoats
of white and jade, wistaria and jasmine,
had smiled suddenly in our faces.

Sudden smiles melt, die like caprices.
This one did. Precious, porcelain joy
fell in a heap of still-shining pieces.

In brackets

Under my balcony nightingales sing,
without feather and without wing,
without wing and without feather.
(Their song is joy at our being together.)

Beyond the chimneys stars are shining:
silver their coat and silver the lining,
silver their lining and silver the coat.
(Golden the warmth of your hand on my throat.)

Far past the stars, a fine moon is dreaming
of lovers who sigh for the light and its gleaming,
of lovers who sigh for the gleam of its light.
(But moon or no moon, our eyes are aye bright.)

My clock is proud of its regular tick.
It knows the moments to chime and click,
It knows the moments to click and chime.
(Could we convince it our love knows no time?)

Don't ask

Don't ask
how much I love you,
when I love you
so much more
than such questions mean.

When we met,
we weren't looking
for each other.
All this love
was unforeseen.

So, accept what is offered
when it's offered
(life *takes*, too).
Take the love, doubt, hate,
reassurance,
and humiliation,
vague frustration.
Take the nights,
black or gold;
take the days,
new or old,

Take the days
till life takes them back,
as it does,
as it will, and we have to -
and we will -
go our different ways.

The common dream

When like the light our lives
with sleep fade in the night,
is there some difference discernible
between our bodies, yours and mine
and all stretched mindless
in a million beds?

And on the resumption of the day
and our activity,
what real distinction can we make
between the bald head
and the other, lustrous,
bent in thought or boredom
in their work and play?

There is no difference.
None.
The million frames are one.
the million brains united willy-nilly
over a common theme:
survival; life -
making the best of it;
erratic attempts at improvement.

Can it be right?
All humanity is served
by a common dream,
and still we fight.

For Roy and Olga

Now that the tide of the mind is turning
on a white, bright confusion of waves,
and the dull, insistent melody of conjecture
has become a single note for me to hold,
I can at long last say
what I have long wished to say,
but lacked the ready words
to fit together.

That if, in passing on,
I meet at least another such as you,
my life will be a life not merely spent.
And I may cling still to my argument
that there are some men who are more than men,
leaving a precious imprint
of warmth and worth
behind them.

When they go,
we mourn their going,
but we do not need to look for them again.

A Roy e Olga

Ora che la marea della mia mente si muta
in una bianca, lucente confusione di onde,
e la triste, insistente melodia d'una decisione
è diventata una nota che devo mantenere,
posso rilassarmi e dire
ciò che da tempo intendevo dire,
ma non trovavo le parole per esprimere:

che sì, nel passar degli anni,
potrò incontrare molti fratelli como voi,
la mia vita sarà una vita non semplicemente spesa.
E posso ancora aggiungere al mio argomento,
che ci sono uomini che sono che uomini
che lasciano il prezioso segno della loro amicizia
dietro di sè. Essi sono andati -
rimpiango il loro partire, ma
no ho bisogno di cercarli ancora.

(translated by Olga MacGregor Hastie)

Lunch

In a small Greek café
we sat having lunch.
Even through the closed windows
I could feel the air
heavy with thunder,
like a fat man in a hammock,
forcing it down.
At our table, though,
all was light and fragrance.
We ate taramosalata
and stuffed vine leaves -
soft and succulent in our mouths,
like a loved body.

You told me not to smoke.

The waiter,
gruff and professional,
with bored, beady eyes,
didn't notice the fragrant light
at our table;
only noticed we were taking
too long over our food.

Were there other people there?

He brought us a fine red wine,
which queened it over the food.

You told me not to smoke,
but I lit a cigarette,
and yet
I didn't want it.

I wanted to look at you.
your eyes in mine,
your mouth smiling, recounting
adventures of youth,
your blue shirt.

Then suddenly, I felt it
Hurt.

(There *were* other people there.)

A wonderful sequence of feeling,
of hurt, thrill,
exquisite pain,
trembling in the weighed-down air,
desire,
a terrible desire,
burning into my heart
and arms,
longing to have you in them.

There were other people there,
but their hubbub was nothing
against the loud noise
in my being.

And I could only stare
at myself in you
and wonder,
and wish we were not there.

Out of the coffee bar

We sat in another quaint new coffee bar.
Walls and weird chairs cried out 'contemporary!'
The unconcealed lights were bare and bleak.
There was a smell of coffee and meals cooking.
And the coffee was weak.

In the street we almost managed to reassume
peace, in spite of cars and people on the pavement,
and the London feeling of awful vastness
but little room to think.

Then, within a moment, we were in the dark.
Lamp lights were only stars beyond the trees.
The paths were cleaned bare of humanity.

You brought me into the park, silently,
out of the worldliness and noise.
The fine feeling of not having to talk
that descends at moments on true friends,
remains settled softly about our shoulders.
And not having to talk,
I feel your closeness to me.

My house, made yours

In the house made mine
by all I have accumulated in it
I walk this morning slowly
from room to room,
smelling and sensing,
thinking and finding
it is no longer mine.

I pick up trinkets: cold and smooth
as your hands are on a windy day.
A new aura surrounds my books
touched and perused by your mind.
The carpet has felt your feet,
this cushion, your head,
the bed has heard your heart beating.

I open the windows wide to allow
a cool wind to suck away
the stale languor diffused by sleep.
But then,
recalling the scent of love lies there,
I seal off the place again
and sit
at peace in a chair a bit,
idly stroking my hair,
savouring your present absence
in my house, made yours
through the opening and closing
of two doors.

Thought over my parapet

I could love you
because of the compassion
that you do not talk of having;
or for that inability
to put things into words,
your silent eloquence.
And I could love, remembering
your many faults (mine outnumber them
ten to one).

I could hate you, though,
for helping me forget sometimes
to have to think,
then forcing me back
with a sickening swiftness
to face the horrific, constant need
to keep my head in a senseless world.
If I considered for long, too,
how petty is my method
of life-contriving
against your greater one,
I might be able to hate you.

I could hate you,
But I love you.

Atmospherics

A few motions, a look, a bang of the door,
commonplace tokens,
trivial, not worth remembering,
have bred something strange
out of compatibility.
Yet this is somehow strong
and lasting longer
than cavern echoes, or the smell
of a bouquiniste's oldest book.

And look, I never saw just how oddly consistent
were these strip lights suspended over my head,
or noticed the dust
standing tip-toe on the carpet.
Now I am aware of this, and more.

You yawn noisily, as when alone at bedtime.
But shall I sleep tonight, I wonder,
after this souring moment
of thunder to my peace of mind,
darkening the sunny corner
of our morning,
troubling me like a curse?

What is worse, this is so trivial,
not worth remembering.

Plea for moderation

When it was just a question of toleration
and convincing myself quickly that this was love
and convincing you, who loved me beyond doubt,
sudden self-consciousness shook my deceit.
But it was soon strangled.
I enjoyed even the melodrama
of mingled emotions.

Then we knew at least one brand of happiness:
laughter over my insincere stupidity;
looking at things together;
arguing over colours of clothes in shop windows,
huddling close in the cold weather like two two lone wolves.
And do you recall our saying of people:
"Poor wretched fools, mostly,
trusting the hard-lined face of independence"?
(Our minds erased those features, perhaps with pencil..)
In these imagined-lovesick moments I marvelled
that still I was allowed sound nightly sleep.

And now I know in a second of scrubbed-white clarity
I love you. Not with the teaspoon-measured love
of couples in suburbia on Sundays.

I do not even look at you, nor have to.
But I grow tired,
the fingers of my concentration, sticky,
for I perceive that
knowing as yet no boundary, this sensation
is born of the one I felt
when I was adored once, and I but liked -
suffocation stealthily approaching,
at times hot hate and, very seldom, pity.

How do I word my plea for moderation?

After : Before

Listen. can you hear something?

What is it, love?

Listen. There it is again.

Oh it is only your heart beating; and mine.

No, no. It is something more.

What, then?

I can make out a melody.

Ah. Is it sharp-sweet, insistent yet elusive?

Yes. Yes.

A haunting phrase it would be pleasant to hum -

Yes -

- that would make a perfect theme for a symphony?

So you hear it, too?

I have heard it already, many times.

No, my love. It is a new song. Our song.

No, dear one. It is an old song
listened to on a different pillow.

My pillow is wet under your cheek. You are weeping.

The song does not lose its poignancy.

If it makes you unhappy, do not let us listen.

We have no choice. If we escape the music
still we think the words.

Words?

They describe the making of love as a paradox
of defeat and conquest.
You conquer, I conquer. We are both defeated.
Our struggle culminates in a joint supremacy,
anti-climax impairing the impact of crisis.
Each victor feels discontent, each vanquished humiliation.
and time, recommencing, brings in appropriate doubts.

Darling, darling, hush.
That sounds so metaphysical.
How does this sad song end?

It does not end.
Unreasonable dreams come with the first caress.
After the last, there is still less place for reason.
And the next fight, the new first,
we await with irrational impatience.

Bare thorn

In my garden before the morning
I pulled a rose of blood,
that is the essence of love and wonder
and thus the essence of good.

I wrapped the rose in a silver tissue,
soft for a flower's bed,
pleased with its power of preservation
of such a delicate head.

And the flower travelled the country with me
as far as my waiting room.
Freed of its pillow of silver paper
it glowed blood red in the gloom.

The gloom of evening spread about us,
the grey of the silence grew;
your silence grew in a womb of sadness,
and the rose spilled blood, and knew.

Loitering hours went by, and we waited,
seeming to wait in vain.
But in my room before the morning
you had appeared again.

The blood of the rose trembled to see you,
and mine trembled with fear,
for the flower I brought you had no meaning:
it took you too long to come near.

How, when you left me, my mistrust growing,
could I give you the rose of blood
that is the essence of love and wonder,
and thus the essence of good?

Now my heart before the morning
is nothing but forlorn,
and like the rose, bereft of petals,
my love is a bare thorn.

Life

Spare us the hypocrites, the annullers of truth;
those who bear ogre grievances
against all but themselves;
those who amass regrets, extract a depraved thrill
out of adversity;
those who carry their umbrellas through the years
for fear of rain.

Or, if out of charity, we must accept them,
save us at least from their common malady:
the maltreatment of life.

* * *

Do you see life -
there, in front of you -
in a dream that is bright
to the point of garishness?
Can you hear her lusty voice,
her laughter jumping?
See, and hear, and consider,
and love this life,

She is a harlot possessed of virgin sincerity,
unashamed of her ways - enjoying them, rather.
She can weep tears, it is true,
and hum sad songs
(experience has taught her
that tragedy lies behind all happiness).
But with a resilience that quickens the affection
she is laughing towards us again,
sighing for notice.
Her generous arms are open to the world.
Run, run to them.
And I'll run with you.

1962

The growth of illusion

I

I was conceived in January -
in England a cold, drab month
when the four walls symbolic of home
enclose even rebels in the false security
they escape from in summer;
they submit for the winter, though, willingly,
to the hypnotic dangers
of fireside warmth and hot drinks on the hearth.

I imagine myself conceived
in a long, snow-drowned evening
when my parents decided the best place was bed.
Did they lie close for comfort's sake
or because the mattress was narrow?
Was their proximity just a convenience,
allowing whispers to pass unheard next door?
Was I borne out of boredom?
Was my conception automatic, accidental,
or fruit of a human curiosity?
I shall never know, for I cannot presume
to ask why they made me exist.

The seed that was me
swelled through the dregs of that first winter.
By spring I had grown
to the size of a physical ache.
In summer, the discomfort of heat with weight
must have made my mother curse me.

And then, at the end of October,
I was allowed out
into a world
of livid skies and sunlight,
and an earth covered
in the brown and orange droppings
of trees apathetic about leaf-bearing;
wanting a rest before spring buds tormented them.

II

Without illusions I passed from my mother's womb.
At least at that time, untaught and innocent,
there was some excuse for having them.

Now I can no longer claim an excuse
in ignorance,
illusions nonetheless live in me,
undeniable, as I, three months prior to birth.

In this twenty-eighth autumn of mine
I see on the same earth
its crunchy carpet of amber;
and the trees, stark, stoic, waiting
for next March and a new sublimation;
and the pallid sun, a ghost of June's,
far from faded completely.

Alas

How nice to be a great man,
how nice to be simple;
how fine to have a domed brow,
how fair to wear a dimple.

How rare to be a rich man,
how big to be a broker.
How great to be a small child
playing with a poker.

How grand to be a saintly man,
looked-up to and revered.
How interesting, the small or mean,
the weak or meek or weird.

Alas...

(With Bill Price, 1965)

God is love

God is, love,
the one you turn to, they say,
when the world gets in the way.
Which way
do you turn, though -
left? right? centre?
Is God a political giant?

No.
He is the true Coalition.

Down to married life

The best mornings

The best mornings are those that start with birds singing: country birds with clear, reassuring voices.

If only lives could start like country mornings in, say, June, as now here in Ropley.

The dawn comes, the sun smoothly and painlessly breaks the skin of the night sky, and there is light. Then the birds, again with a rupturing process, stir in the trees and begin their fierce and sweet breaking of the sound barrier of dawn.

One lies in bed, and wonders at it all. Light, music, peace.

Soon the peace is broken, too, for the babies stir in their cots. As the birds, a little before, twitched their soft feathers in awareness of the new day.

Ben starts his chirruping first, kicking his long, fat legs in time. Angus, disturbed by Ben, mutters 'baba' in his low, melodious voice and gradually, unwillingly, joins the chorus.

Sound and light increase. The sun makes a mockery of the thin, print curtains. The babies find their voices. The central heating turns itself on responsibly, with a roar. Then I get up, and there are the breakfast sounds. And smells. And everything.

Yes, that's how all days should begin. And lives, too?

Few lives do start so well. Those that do, often peter out in a cloudy afternoon. Isn't that right?

It is those of us who are given a second life, who experience this kind of morning-break. Those of us who struggle on, 'still bent to make some port he knows not where', as Arnold wrote; we who blindly hope for the best, cliché-binding our actions, sometimes win a morning like this. I am one of them, and the marvellous truth of it lightens my step, and sweetens my dreams every day and night of my life.

Ropley
Summer, 1969

A cocky song

Whom do we tell
when we feel right down,
down at the bottom
of the great big well
of slimy, echoing, dank despair?
Who would care?

God?
On His cloud,
cluttered up with angels,
and days and days
of unfinished business;
smothering (if he could)
in a dubious shroud
sent Him for Christmas
by gaudy, ageless Lucifer:
the eternal bit of tinsel
tickling God's ear;
weeping in a crowd,

ever growing,
if sinners who can help it, and
sinners who can not?

Husband?
Weighed down by bills,
working on a hundred things,
and a hundred horses,
harassed to confusion?
No room in that head
to take our little sadnesses
(or evenour hopes,
or our fun).
Perish that illusion.

Children?
Asleep In bed,
baby-powdered
deep-dreaming angels,
eight hands clean till dawn,
hearts pure as Irish rain.
They should be able
to make me feel better.
But they would be frightened
if they saw my frowns;
uncertain, unsettled,
if they thought their mother
had up's and down's.
No, I must not show my weeping
to my babies sleeping.

Who, then, who?
Stand on your own two feet, they say,
Well - one, two.

Life's next challenge

One-parent blues

A night fear...

(All children sleeping,
all kitchen things in place,
rubbish gathered and gone outside.
Gloves ready for the morning school departure;
and hats, and scarves
folded neatly, or otherwise,
according to their owners.

My bed turned back.
Letters written,
grants sought,
bills paid - or shelved)...

I am alone,
the last sock sewn,
and now?
What shall I do here?
Who shall I say goodnight to?

Perhaps I feel
not so much fear
as utter loneness.

February, 1981

For Bella, remembering Grandfather

You came home with a story:
you took in your purse to school
to buy a poppy for Remembrance Day.
You slid a pound
into the slot
of the collecting, respecting tin.

Why did they not give you change?

I know, I know -
a pound for a small girl
is a whole fortune.

But, remember:
for one, your grandfather, my father,
gave an eye, an ear, the use of some fingers
and a leg, for war.
He was a peaceful, quiet man.
But the First World War called him,
like many, and he went into it:
blood, sand, mud, death, horror, and more.

Your pound, your well-saved pound....
think of it as cool, soothing ointment
on a burning wound;
think of it as a binding, saving bandage
on a bleeding cut.
Think of it as a soft, soothing nurse's hand
on a fevered brow.

Think of this NOW (although this was in the past,
it will always be in our lives)
as a sweet, calming, shining smile,
like one of yours, my daughter,
when I am sad or cross
or so in need of you.

So much your pound is worth,
beyond value, beyond definition.
Dear Bella,
aren't you glad you gave it,
gave it all?

1979

For Bella, just 11

When I think of you, my daughter,
I see red roses shining through the frost;
the cold air outside Pear Tree Cottage
warmly touches my face.
As I think of you,
I feel your friendly, silky cat, Greenie,
rub gently against my legs.
My Bella,
when I think of you, all other thoughts go,
sadness vanishes,
anger frizzles out.

I am left smiling,
with a kiss in one hand
and a tear in the other.

Life *is* kisses and tears and smiles.
Life is you.

30 November, 1982

Unforthcoming ground

I want a warming fire,
bright orange and yellow flames leaping;
a comfortable chair, soft light,
unblinding blend of sight, and sound, and feeling.
I want a piece of unforthcoming ground.

I need a face, smiling and warm;
one friendly shout; one happy arrival;
someone plonking their luggage down,
glad to be back.

I want my children back.

Where did they go?
Surely, not into the cold snow.
No, I did not guide them there.
I sent them, with love and care,
and tenderness (not always clearly shown,
since I was on my own with them)
to paths considered theirs.

Now they have gone.
They are all struggling past me (into what?).

That is what hurts.
The struggling past me.
Discarding, superseding,
discrediting, belittling,
casually, *en passant.*

How do I cope with that?

September, 1989

On course again

Firework words

Whenever you touch my life
you beautify it
in definable ways.

Wit, clear and sharp
as the moon on darkness,
brightens the lucky days
and eases a trail
of brilliant firework words
behind it.

Not only wit and word.
The feelings are there, too.
Subdued, but deep enough
to be heard.

You can touch my life:
a trembling taper
lights the catherine wheel
which whirs audibly,
and sparks fly,
all ways.

1988

Before the night is out

I am drawing the blinds down,
closing off my life from the outside,
The green of hedges and rose trees
have merged into the darkness of night.
I want to be encased, enfolded,
in the quiet and warmth of my kitchen.

104

I am drawing the blinds down
in more ways than one;
closing my life off, from that of others:
needing to know how much I need them -
how much, to be alone.

It is a need to be alone with my thoughts,
with where I am going, with God,
not selfish aloneness.

No doubt before the night is out,
God, silent, inescapable,
will tell me what to do...

Be alone - use my life for myself?
Stay put? Think valuable thoughts?
Think not of myself, but of others?
Act on that!

Let up those blinds!
Let the glittering moon in.
Tomorrow, let in the sun,
Let others in, too.

God did not say all this,
He put it in my mind,

Thank you, God,

April, 1991

Along the bronzing lanes

Winter came early this year,
In October, with the crops
still not all gathered in.
Bright stars, red dawns, hard frosts
laid waste the last courgettes;
tarnished the final apples with untimely spots.

That is when you left us,
Ros, in that early winter.

Your family mourn,
and I, in my small corner,
mourn you, too.

Then autumn asserted itself,
helping the hardier harvest,
bringing wry cheer to the grieving
in its morning sun,
wanting to hope you live.
(I *know* you live on.)

On a fair morning in November,
I walked with Fred, unleashed,
along the bronzing lanes,
thinking of you, your father, our meetings...
I remembered you saying:
"I like your coat."
"Have it," I offered.
"No, no," you said, "it's yours."
Odd, the remembered things.

Out of the mourning,
in my mind, I see you smile,
somehow secret, quiet, taking all in
(like your father).
I see in my mind's eye,
your smiling face,
framed in a mass of golden hair.
I feel you there
in the bronzing lanes,
And I rejoice for you.

Now you are safe from the busy traffic
of this world,
warm in the arms of God.
We should try not to be sad,
knowing that.

December, 1991

Midnight message to Orlando

Just about twenty-one years ago
I lay in a hard bed
in Dublin's Rotunda Hospital
waiting, desperately,
for you to be born.

(We had already been admitted once.
Not ready, they said.
I crept home,
feeling like a guilty fox.)

The nurses were awful,
unsympathetic to my pains this time.
"Hurry along," they ordered. "PUSH!"

They would not let your father in.
"You wait outside," they said.
"I'll burn this place down," he countered,
"if you don't let me in."
But they didn't.
They stuck out for their routine rights.

Then, around midnight, you were born.
My gynaecologist was not there;
he was dining in Dublin,
not expecting your imminent birth.
Instead, a worried young houseman peered down.
"I've never done this before," he said.
"Don't worry," I whispered,
"it'll be fine."
A quick smile from him,
some spasms from me,
and you were born.

The brick-faced nurses took you
immediately from me,
Your father was hammering at the door.
"What a gem!" they murmured.

During the night,
back in my bed,
I awoke to find a strange man
kneeling beside it.
"Forgive me," my gynaecologist said,
"I didn't think you'd give birth
this night."

What matter. You were born.
Bless the Rotunda, Dublin,
where you came into the world.

12:29 am,
4th December, 1991

The two fires

I have lit fires for you tonight:
two fires,
one in the Rayburn -
a sensible, practical source of heat,
warming not only the kitchen
at Pear Tree Cottage
but all the rooms around it;
heating the water,
toward the joy of a hot bath...
and one in the sitting room...
wound-up newspaper rings,
topped with
Jim Pescod's fine firewood
then (a little later),
with oak and ash logs
from the stacks
in Angus's 'car-buncle'.

The first fire comes to life
obediently, quickly,
in a consistent way.
Why should it not?
Sensible thought
went into the stove's construction,
reflecting, no doubt,
the engineer's own need
to be warm by day, warm at night,
and have hot water.

The second fire,
built to roar (hopefully)
up an open chimney,
is somewhat less predictable
in coming to glowing glory.
There are false starts; fierce, enthusiastic flickers
leading at times nowhere,
at times to a glorious blaze.
This uncertainty
may necessitate paper over the fireplace gap,
to fan the flames.

Your two lives together,
Orlando and Libby,
will be like these two fires:
the one, well designed, foreseeable;
the other, less so,
needing attention, coaxing,
and the latter will be the great challenge.

So,
may the Rayburn
and the open fire
(like those lit each day
in the cottage)
be your fires,
and warm the way
throughout your lives.

November, 1993

ACKNOWLEDGEMENTS

A number of poems in this anthology have already been broadcast or published, in English, French, Spanish and Italian. They include the following:

Plea for Moderation   (*The New Station,* Sydney, Australia, January-February, 1959)

Brown touch   (Radiodiffusion Télévision Française, Paris Far-Eastern Service, 1957)

For Michael   (*The Prairie Poet,* Charleston, Illinois, Spring, 1958)
(*Thirty More Poems,* West Sussex Federation of Women's Institutes, 1991)

A method of forgiveness   (*Poesía Española,* Madrid, No.77, May, 1959)
(Spanish version)

Shirt music   (*Caravan,* Hawkeye Poetry Magazine, Iowa, Vol. 5, No.4, September-October, 1959)

Peace   (*The Prairie Poet,* Fall, 1959)

Bare thorn   (*The Prairie Poet,* Winter, 1959)

For my brothers   (*Caravan,* December, 1960)
(for Roy and Olga)

Dualogue on the Point   (*Saltire Review,* Edinburgh, No.23)
      Spanish Version -   (*Poesía Espanola,* Madrid, No.77, May, 1959)
(*Scribe,* Emerson College, Boston, Mass., Vol. VIII, No.2, Winter, 1991)